EQAO Grade 3 Language Test Prep

—— Teacher Guide ——

Written by Ruth Solski

RUTH SOLSKI was an educator for 30 years. She has written many educational resources and is the founder of S&S Learning Materials. As a writer, her main goal is to provide teachers with a useful tool that they can implement in their classrooms to bring the joy of learning to children.

Published in Canada by:
On The Mark Press
15 Dairy Avenue, Napanee, Ontario, K7R 1M4
www.onthemarkpress.com

Funded by the
Government
of Canada

Canada

Table of Contents

About This Book

This book was created to help Grade 3 students prepare for the EQAO Language Assessment test. Tests 1 – 9 have been designed to be very similar to the actual test the students will be taking. Many of the questions are asked in a similar way so that students can get familiar with the questioning format. Students will encounter different types of reading experiences including fiction, nonfiction, diagrams, and instructions. They will be asked to read sentences, paragraphs, and stories and then answer corresponding questions about the content or structure. There is also plenty of writing practice as students are asked to write sentences, paragraphs, and stories and answer questions featuring essential writing skills.

Test 10 is a bonus test to give students extra practice with specific language skills. There is no particular sequence to the tests. They can be used in whatever order you choose to fit your students needs.

SSG111   ISBN: 9781487704001 © On The Mark Press

An Unexpected Visitor

My brother Andy and I were excited! When school finished in June, we were going to northern Ontario to spend the summer. Our grandfather lived there on a small farm.

We had visited there a few times but this was awesome! Two months of living "in the bush" as Mom called it. And Gramps was so much fun! He was a real woodsman in our eyes.

We arrived in Moosonee after a very long train ride. Gramps was there to pick us up. We loaded our suitcases into the back of his old pickup truck.

"Sure glad you boys are here," Gramps said. "I have a lot of things planned to do. And I need some help fixing up around the barn."

Gramps' farm was really a cabin with a barn and a few acres of land. It was down a long road and we didn't see any other houses nearby.

"Do you have many visitors, Gramps?" Andy asked.

SSG111 ISBN: 9781487704001 © On The Mark Press

"Nope," he replied. Gramps could spin a great story but he didn't believe in useless talk.

We were exhausted from our long trip. We unloaded our belongings then had a snack. We decided to go to bed early. Our bedroom faced the woods and we could hear all kinds of animal sounds. Sometime in the middle of the night, Andy woke me up.

"Look out the window!" he whispered. There stood the biggest moose we had ever seen! It was quietly staring at us. Just checking us out, I guess. It stood there a while longer. Finally, it turned and wandered off into the woods.

We had just had our first "visitor."

7

8

9

10

4

SSG111   ISBN: 9781487704001 © On The Mark Press

An Unexpected Visitor: Questions

1. What does Gramps mean when he says, "Sure glad you boys are here," in paragraph 4?

   ○ He misses seeing the boys.

   ○ He is lonely and glad for the company.

   ○ He needs some help fixing things around the barn.

   ○ He wishes the boys lived with him.

2. What is the main purpose of paragraph 5?

   ○ to explain why the boys wanted to visit Gramps

   ○ to describe the farm where Gramps lives

   ○ to tell about the unexpected visitor

   ○ to explain what Gramps had planned for the summer

3. What does the word "exhausted" mean in paragraph 8?

   ○ extremely tired

   ○ very excited

   ○ kind of sleepy

   ○ extremely hungry

4. What does the word "visitor" refer to in paragraph 10?

   ○ Gramps' neighbour

   ○ Andy

   ○ Mom

   ○ a moose

An Unexpected Visitor: Questions

5. Write what happens in the story before and after the events listed below. Use details from the text to support your answers.

    a. _____

    _____

    _____

    b. Gramps picks the boys up in his old pickup truck.

    c. The boys unload their belongings and have a snack before going to bed early.

    d. The boys wake up to see a huge moose staring through the window at them.

    e. _____

    _____

    _____

6. Explain why you think the boys were excited to spend the summer with their grandfather. Use details from the text and your own ideas to support your answer.

    _____

    _____

    _____

    _____

    _____

    _____

    _____

SSG111   ISBN: 9781487704001 © On The Mark Press

Writing a Paragraph

7. Write a paragraph about a summer vacation that you would like to take. Describe the place and what you would like to do there.

Ideas for my paragraph

_____

_____

_____

_____

_____

_____

_____

Write your paragraph on the next page.

This page will not be scored.

Writing a Paragraph

Write your paragraph here. Remember to check your spelling, grammar and punctuation.

_____

Do not write in this area.

SSG111   ISBN: 9781487704001 © On The Mark Press

Writing Multiple Choice

8. What is the best way to join the following sentences?

   The school is named Butler Acres.

   The school is made of brick.

   The school is on the corner of Maple and Birch streets.

   ○ Butler Acres school is brick and it sits on the corner of Maple and Birch streets.

   ○ The school named Butler Acres is made of brick it is on the corner of Maple and Birch streets.

   ○ Butler Acres is on the corner of Maple and Birch, it is made of brick.

   ○ The brick school is on the corner it is named Butler Acres.

9. Choose the word or words that correctly complete the sentence.

   Tomorrow, I _____ to visit my favorite aunt.

   ○ went

   ○ have been

   ○ will go

   ○ did go

10. Choose the sentence that correctly joins the words "do not."

   ○ I dont know Sara very well.

   ○ I dont' know Sara very well.

   ○ I donot know Sara very well.

   ○ I don't know Sara very well.

Writing Multiple Choice

11. You can make most singular nouns into plural nouns by adding either an **s**, an **es**, or an **ies**. Write the plural form of each of the following nouns.

a. library _____

b. branch _____

c. lady _____

d. lamp _____

e. soldier _____

f. address _____

g. country _____

12. Which of the following sentences is correctly written?

○ The three babies blankets were each a different colour.

○ The three babys blankets were each a different colour.

○ The three babies' blankets were each a different colour.

○ The three babie's blankets were each a different colour.

13. Which sentence does not belong in the following paragraph?

(a.) Skateboard parks have rules so kids will be safe. (b.) Skateboards come in many colors. (c.) Kids must wear kneepads and gloves. (d.) They must wear helmets on their heads. (e.) Skateboarding can be fun if you obey the rules.

○ Sentence b.

○ Sentence c.

○ Sentence d.

○ Sentence e.

SSG111   ISBN: 9781487704001 © On The Mark Press

Bears Just Want to Have Fun!

It was a beautiful fall day. Mother Bear and her cubs were on an outing. Mother Bear plodded along a path in the woods. Her two little cubs were right behind her.

1

Mother Bear spotted an old rotting log. With a push of her big strong paw, she turned the log over. Hundreds of bugs scurried to get away. But Mother Bear and her cubs were too fast for them. Soon the bugs were all gobbled up!

2

Then Mother Bear noticed some bushes that were full of berries. She began to gobble up the berries as fast as she could. The cubs were busy munching too. When the berries were gone, Mother Bear stood up on her hind legs and began to sniff the air.

3

The cubs stood up and began to sniff the air too. What were those wonderful smells they wondered? Soon they spied something that made their mouths water. A picnic!

4

The Greenberg family had just pulled into a roadside rest stop. They were on a long trip to visit family up north. Mom and Dad thought a picnic would be a good idea. The children started running around while Mom and Dan unloaded the food.

5

Soon the table was full of sandwiches, pickles, boiled eggs, fruit, and cupcakes. Milk and juice were in the cooler. Just as Mom was calling everyone to the table, the family spotted the bears.

6

"Run! Run fast! Get into the car!" yelled Dad. The family scrambled to safety just in time! They watched from the car as the bears started to eat.

7

Mother bear and her cubs had a wonderful feast eating all the goodies on the table. She even managed to tear open the milk and juice boxes.

8

But Mother Bear and her cubs were puzzled as they looked at the car. Why had those silly creatures made such a fuss?

9

SSG111   ISBN: 9781487704001 © On The Mark Press

Bears Just Want to Have Fun! Questions

1. What does the word "plodded" mean as used in paragraph 1?

   ○ to stumble

   ○ to move in a slow, heavy way

   ○ to move quickly

   ○ to work in a slow, steady way

2. Why does Mother Bear turn over the rotting log?

   ○ to move it out of the way

   ○ to show her cubs how to move a log

   ○ to get to the bugs underneath it

   ○ to get to the berries underneath it

3. What is the main purpose of paragraph 6?

   ○ to describe the picnic food that was on the table

   ○ to tell why the bears were hungry

   ○ to describe the Greenberg family

   ○ to tell why the family was having a picnic

4. Where do paragraphs 5 – 9 take place?

   ○ in the family car

   ○ deep in the woods

   ○ in the berry bushes

   ○ at a roadside rest stop

Bears Just Want to Have Fun! Questions

5. Explain the main purpose of the bears' outing. Use information from the text to support your answer.

_____

_____

_____

_____

_____

_____

6. Explain why Dad yells "Run! Run fast! Get into the car!" Use information from the text and your own ideas to support your answer.

_____

_____

_____

_____

_____

_____

_____

SSG111   ISBN: 9781487704001 © On The Mark Press

Bears Just Want to Have Fun! Questions

7. Name two things that happened after Mother Bear stood up on her hind legs to sniff the air. Use information from the text to support your answer.

_____

_____

_____

_____

_____

_____

8. Do you think the family did the right thing when they saw the bears? Give a reason for your answer. Use your own ideas to support your answer.

_____

_____

_____

_____

_____

_____

_____

Writing a Paragraph

9. Write a paragraph about your favorite kind of picnic. Explain who is at the picnic and where the picnic takes place. Describe what kind of food is at the picnic.

Ideas for my paragraph

_____

_____

_____

_____

_____

_____

_____

Write your paragraph on the next page.

This page will not be scored.

SSG111   ISBN: 9781487704001 © On The Mark Press

Writing a Paragraph

Write your paragraph here. Remember to check your spelling, grammar and punctuation.

_____

_____

_____

_____

_____

_____

_____

_____

_____

Do not write in this area.

Writing Multiple Choice

10. Choose the word that best joins these sentences.

    I was walking through the park.
    A bird landed on my shoulder.

    ○ because

    ○ when

    ○ with

    ○ but

11. Choose the sentence that is written correctly.

    ○ Get up! yelled Clark. "Youll be late for school."

    ○ "Get up," yelled Clark! "You'll be late for school."

    ○ "Get up!" yelled Clark. You'll be late for school.

    ○ "Get up!" yelled Clark. "You'll be late for school."

12. Choose the best closing sentence for this paragraph.

    Mama tigers can have between two and five tiger cubs born at one time.
    The cubs each weigh about three pounds at birth. They stay with their mom
    until they are about three years old. _____

    ○ Cubs start hunting with their mom at six weeks old.

    ○ Tigers live mostly in India and Southeast Asia.

    ○ Then the cubs go off on their own.

    ○ A male tiger can weigh up to 700 pounds.

SSG111   ISBN: 9781487704001 © On The Mark Press

Writing Sentences

Rewrite each of the following sentences using the correct punctuation.

13. Help I cant swim

_____

14. Lets go to the movies said Jane

_____

15. Shouldnt you try to get home before dark

_____

16. Maya went to the store to buy eggs milk cheese and bread.

_____

17. Mrs Wilson asked Could you please take my picture

_____

18. Yes Jackie you can go skating tomorrow

_____

What is a Mammal?

Common Traits

Mammals are an interesting and diverse group of animals. Humans belong to this animal group. To be in the mammal group an animal must share some common traits.

❶

- Mammals must feed their young milk produced by the mother.

❷

- All mammals are warm-blooded, which means their body temperature stays the same whether it is hot or cold outside. Their bodies burn energy to maintain a constant temperature.

❸

- Mammals have hair or fur on their bodies. The hair or fur helps keep the animals warm and can protect them against germs. Some animals use their fur as camouflage to keep them safe.

❹

- All mammals are vertebrates. They have backbones and an internal skeleton. They breathe with lungs. They have four major systems: circulatory, digestive, nervous, and respiratory.

❺

Reproduction/Young

Mammals are born live except for the platypus and the echidna. These two mammals hatch from eggs. Many kinds of mammal babies need lots of care and attention when they are born. They cannot feed themselves or protect themselves from danger. They need ongoing care for several years to survive into adulthood.

❻

SSG111   ISBN: 9781487704001

Humans, elephants, horses, cows, and hippopotamuses usually have one baby at a time. Pigs, cats, dogs, and rabbits often have a litter of several babies at a time.

7

Some mammals, like horses, are born able to walk; their eyes and ears are open, and their skin is covered with hair. Other mammals, like mice, are barely able to crawl; their skin is hairless, and their eyes and ears are still shut.

8

Koalas, kangaroos, wombats, and possums are marsupial mammals. Marsupials give birth to live young that are not very well developed. Shortly after the baby is born it crawls into its mother's pouch. It will stay there for the next few weeks until it's able to go out on its own.

9

Habitats

Mammals live in many different types of environments all around the world. These environments are their habitats. They live in jungles, forests, deserts, mountains, grasslands, and oceans.

10

They have adapted to be able to survive intense tropical heat and freezing arctic temperatures.

11

What is a Mammal? Questions

1. In paragraph 3, the term "warm-blooded" refers to

   ○ the mammals' body temperature.

   ○ the outside temperature.

   ○ the mammals' personality.

   ○ the amount of energy mammals burn.

2. What is the main purpose of paragraph 4?

   ○ to explain how mammals keep warm

   ○ to explain why mammals have hair or fur on their bodies

   ○ to explain how mammals stay safe

   ○ to explain why mammals have germs

3. What is the meaning of the word "traits" as it is used in paragraph 1?

   ○ things that make mammals human

   ○ reasons that there are lots of different mammals

   ○ mammals that feed their young milk

   ○ qualities that belong to and help to identify all mammals

4. Name the mammals that hatch from eggs.

   ○ marsupials

   ○ platypus and echidna

   ○ elephants and kangaroos

   ○ mice and rabbits

SSG111   ISBN: 9781487704001 © On The Mark Press

What is a Mammal? Questions

5. What conclusion can be made about mammals in paragraph 6?

    ○ All baby mammals are vertebrates.

    ○ Baby mammals can take care of themselves.

    ○ Most baby mammals will die if they are not cared for.

    ○ All baby mammals have hair when they are born.

6. In paragraph 9, what is special about baby marsupials?

    ○ They spend several weeks in their mother's pouch.

    ○ They are born hairless.

    ○ They are able to walk when they are born.

    ○ They are part of a litter.

7. Explain why the animal photos are helpful to this story. Use your own ideas to support your answer.

    _____

    _____

    _____

    _____

    _____

    _____

    _____

What is a Mammal? Questions

8. Compare baby horses and baby mice. How are they alike and how are they different? Use information from the text and your own ideas to support your answer.

_____

_____

_____

_____

_____

_____

_____

9. Describe how some mammals have to adapt to live in their habitats. Use information from the text and your own ideas to support your answer.

_____

_____

_____

_____

_____

_____

_____

SSG111   ISBN: 9781487704001 © On The Mark Press

Writing a Paragraph

10. Horses, dogs, cats, cows, sheep, rabbits and hamsters are all mammals. Choose one of these animals and write a paragraph about it. Explain some of the things that you know to be true about that animal.

Ideas for my paragraph

_____

_____

_____

_____

_____

_____

_____

Write your paragraph on the next page.

This page will not be scored.

SSG111   ISBN: 9781487704001 © On The Mark Press

Writing a Paragraph

Write your paragraph here. Remember to check your spelling, grammar and punctuation.

_____

_____

_____

_____

_____

_____

_____

_____

_____

Do not write in this area.

SSG111   ISBN: 9781487704001 © On The Mark Press

Writing Multiple Choice

11. Choose the words that correctly complete the sentence.

    Sam _____ that book five years ago _____ he still likes to read it.

    ○ buys/but

    ○ can buy/when

    ○ bought/but

    ○ will buy/then

12. Choose the sentence that is written correctly.

    ○ "When the class is over, let's go outside," said Meg.

    ○ When the class is over let's go outside, said Meg.

    ○ "When the class is over lets go outside," said Meg.

    ○ When the class is over lets go outside said Meg.

13. Choose the best order to make a paragraph using the following sentences.

    a. Explorers have found very old shipwrecks at the bottom of the ocean.

    b. This has helped us to learn about our past.

    c. For hundreds of years, tropical storms and hurricanes in the Atlantic Ocean have caused trouble for ships.

    d. These shipwrecks often have old cargo that the ships were carrying.

    ○ d, c, a, b

    ○ c, a, d, b

    ○ b, d, c, a

    ○ a, b, d, c

Main Parts of an Airplane

Airplanes are heavier than air. To overcome this, they have been designed with many parts that each have a specific task. When these parts are working together, airplanes are able to take off, land, and fly.

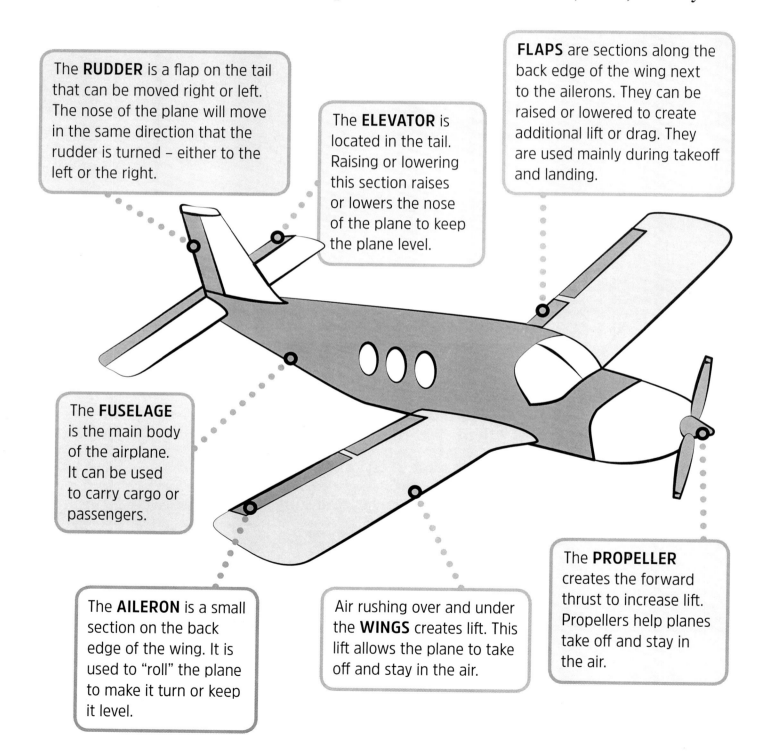

The **RUDDER** is a flap on the tail that can be moved right or left. The nose of the plane will move in the same direction that the rudder is turned – either to the left or the right.

The **ELEVATOR** is located in the tail. Raising or lowering this section raises or lowers the nose of the plane to keep the plane level.

FLAPS are sections along the back edge of the wing next to the ailerons. They can be raised or lowered to create additional lift or drag. They are used mainly during takeoff and landing.

The **FUSELAGE** is the main body of the airplane. It can be used to carry cargo or passengers.

The **AILERON** is a small section on the back edge of the wing. It is used to "roll" the plane to make it turn or keep it level.

Air rushing over and under the **WINGS** creates lift. This lift allows the plane to take off and stay in the air.

The **PROPELLER** creates the forward thrust to increase lift. Propellers help planes take off and stay in the air.

SSG111   ISBN: 9781487704001 © On The Mark Press

Main Parts of an Airplane: Questions

1. What does the diagram of the airplane show?

   ○ the parts of the propeller

   ○ how the airplane takes off

   ○ how to land the airplane

   ○ the parts of the airplane

2. In the diagram, where are the **rudder** and the **elevator** located?

   ○ at the front of the plane

   ○ on the wings of the plane

   ○ at the back of the plane

   ○ near the propellers

3. What part of the plane carries the passengers?

   ○ fuselage

   ○ rudder

   ○ wing

   ○ propeller

4. Which two parts of the plane help it take off and stay in the air?

   ○ ailerons and elevator

   ○ flaps and rudder

   ○ propellers and wings

   ○ fuselage and wings

Main Parts of an Airplane: Questions

5. Explain how the **rudder** helps the plane to turn right or left. Use information from the text to support your answer.

_____

_____

_____

_____

_____

_____

6. Explain why using the **flaps** of the plane help during takeoff and landing. Use information from the text to support your answer.

_____

_____

_____

_____

_____

_____

SSG111   ISBN: 9781487704001 © On The Mark Press

Writing a Story

7. Write a scary short story. To help you get started, choose some of the story starter ideas listed in the graphic organizer below. Add your own ideas to complete your story.

Characters
- a wolf
- an 8-year-old girl
- a 12-year-old boy
- a rescue team

Setting
- a dark, windy night
- deep in the woods
- a large cave
- a small ledge

Plot
- someone gets lost
- a sudden lightning storm
- an accident happens
- a stranger appears

Fill in the blanks with your ideas to help organize your story idea.

Title: _____

Problem: _____

_____

Important Event: _____

_____

Conclusion: _____

_____

Writing a Story

Write your story here. Remember to check your spelling, grammar, and punctuation.

_____

(Title here)

_____

_____

_____

_____

_____

_____

_____

_____

_____

_____

_____

_____

_____

_____

SSG111   ISBN: 9781487704001 © On The Mark Press

Writing a Story

Continue your story here.

_____

_____

_____

_____

_____

_____

_____

_____

_____

_____

_____

_____

_____

_____

_____

Writing Multiple Choice

8. Which sentence does not belong in the following paragraph?

   Tropical rain forests have more types of plants and animals than anywhere else. More than half of the world's plant and animal species live there. It rains almost everyday. Most of these animals and plants can't be found anywhere else.

   ○ Tropical rain forests have more types of plants and animals than anywhere else.

   ○ More than half of the world's plant and animal species live there.

   ○ It rains almost everyday.

   ○ Most of these animals and plants can't be found anywhere else.

9. Choose the word that best starts the following sentence.

   _____ **Andy left for vacation, he asked his neighbor to take care of his dog.**

   ○ After

   ○ Although

   ○ Before

   ○ Where

 SSG111   ISBN: 9781487704001 © On The Mark Press

Life Cycle of a Monarch Butterfly

a A monarch butterfly starts life as an embryo growing inside a tiny, round, soft-shelled egg. The mother leaves after she lays her eggs.

b Four to six days later the egg hatches and a small wormlike creature called a larva is born. The larva has to survive on its own.

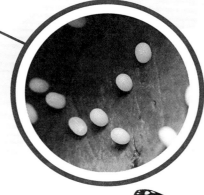

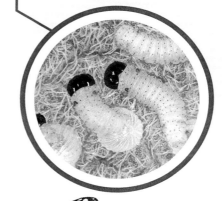

e Once the butterfly body is fully formed, it starts to break out of the cocoon. When it is fully out of the cocoon, it is an adult butterfly.

d The caterpillar forms a cocoon and becomes a pupa. It will stay inside the cocoon for another 14 days. During this time, the caterpillar's tissues breakdown and the adult butterfly body structure is formed.

c The larva or caterpillar eats constantly and grows quickly. It sheds its skin several times as it gets bigger. After about 14 days, the caterpillar is ready for a big change.

SSG111   ISBN: 9781487704001 © On The Mark Press

Life Cycle of a Monarch Butterfly: Questions

1. In paragraph A, what do the words "tiny, round, soft-shelled" describe?

   ○ monarch butterflies

   ○ butterfly pupa

   ○ butterfly embryo

   ○ butterfly egg

2. What can you tell about the larva by looking at photo b. and photo c.?

   ○ It will be a butterfly soon.

   ○ Its appearance changes as it grows and sheds its skin.

   ○ The cocoon is starting to form.

   ○ The butterfly will be orange and black.

3. What does the word "constantly" mean in paragraph C?

   ○ never

   ○ once in awhile

   ○ all the time

   ○ sometimes

4. After the mother butterfly lays her eggs, how long does it take for the eggs to hatch?

   ○ four to six days

   ○ 14 days

   ○ one month

   ○ 48 hours

SSG111   ISBN: 9781487704001 © On The Mark Press

Life Cycle of a Monarch Butterfly: Questions

5. When does a caterpillar become a pupa?

   ○ before the cocoon is formed

   ○ when the mother lays her eggs

   ○ after the cocoon is formed

   ○ before the larva is born

6. What is the last thing to happen before the pupa becomes an adult butterfly?

   ○ It starts to form a cocoon.

   ○ It breaks out of the cocoon.

   ○ It becomes a caterpillar.

   ○ It eats constantly.

7. Explain what is happening in photos d. and e. Use details from the text and information from the photos to support your answer.

   _____

   _____

   _____

   _____

   _____

   _____

   _____

   _____

Writing a Paragraph

8. Write a paragraph that tells some of the ways that you have changed since you were a baby.

Ideas for my paragraph

_____

_____

_____

_____

_____

_____

_____

_____

_____

_____

Write your paragraph on the next page.

This page will not be scored.

SSG111   ISBN: 9781487704001 © On The Mark Press

Writing a Paragraph

Write your paragraph here. Remember to check your spelling, grammar, and punctuation.

_____

_____

_____

_____

_____

_____

_____

_____

_____

_____

_____

Do not write in this area.

SSG111   ISBN: 9781487704001 © On The Mark Press

Writing Multiple Choice

9. Choose the sentence that best completes this paragraph.

   Gorillas build sleeping platforms out of branches. They build the platform part way up a tree. The mother gorilla and her baby sleep up on the platform.

   ○ The next day they are off to find food.

   ○ The father gorilla makes his bed on the ground.

   ○ It gets cold at night in the jungle.

   ○ Morning comes early in the jungle.

10. What is the best way to join the following sentences?

    Our town has fireworks on New Years Eve.
    We like to watch the fireworks.
    We don't like the noise of the fireworks.

    ○ We like to watch the fireworks in our town on New Years Eve, but we don't like the noise.

    ○ Our town has fireworks on New Years Eve and we don't like the noise.

    ○ We like the fireworks, we do not like the noise.

    ○ It is noisy in our town on New Years Eve and we like the fireworks.

11. Which of the following sentences makes an exclamation?

    ○ Do you think it will snow tomorrow?

    ○ I like to take the train when I travel.

    ○ That is the most gorgeous sunset I have ever seen!

    ○ Wash your hands before you eat.

SSG111   ISBN: 9781487704001 © On The Mark Press

Writing Multiple Choice

12. Choose the words that correctly complete this sentence.

    Yesterday, Melissa's aunt _____ **her** _____ **movies.**

    ○ take / to

    ○ taken / at

    ○ taked / on

    ○ took / to

13. Which of the following sentences gives a command?

    ○ Why don't you like me?

    ○ Please stand behind the yellow line.

    ○ That was a fantastic concert!

    ○ My friend and I are going to the hockey game.

14. Choose the best order to make a paragraph using the following sentences.

    a. The wind catches the glider and holds it in the air.
    b. A hang glider looks like a big kite.
    c. The rider runs with the glider and jumps off a hill or a cliff.
    d. The rider is strapped to the glider.

    ○ a, d, c, b

    ○ c, d, b, a

    ○ b, d, c, a

    ○ b, a, c, d

Backyard Sleepover

I thought that spending the summer at my cousin Ben's place would be boring, but it turned out to be pretty exciting after all. Ben lives in a big, old house in the city, with a huge backyard.

In the middle of the yard is a maple tree, where we spent the first week building a treehouse. It wasn't much, just a platform with walls that went up to our knees, and a big flat piece of tin that we used for a roof.

Once the treehouse was finished, we decided to invite Matt, Ben's friend, to spend the night. Matt was the same age as Ben and me but was a lot shorter and really excitable.

As soon as it was dark we collected our sleeping bags and a stash of snacks, then climbed into the treehouse. It was a clear, warm night, with a big white moon hanging in the summer sky.

For the first hour or so everything went really well. We lay there under the stars, finishing up our snacks and telling ghost stories. It was the perfect night for a camp-out. We could even hear an old owl hooting off in the distance.

SSG111   ISBN: 9781487704001 © On The Mark Press

It was then we heard something really creepy – something that sounded like a cat moving slowly up the tree. Scratch . . . scratch . . . scratch.

6

"What's that?" Matt whispers.

7

"Sounds like something's coming up the ladder," Ben whispers back.

8

Matt pulls out his flashlight and shines it over toward the ladder. Then, I swear I could hear this heavy breathing coming from down below.

9

Matt starts to whimper just like a little kid. "It's a ghost!" he whispers. "Let's get out of here!"

10

Now, I don't believe in ghosts, but I could see that even Ben looked a little rattled.

11

"It must be my dog, Winston," says Ben. He then crawls over to the side of the treehouse and peers down the ladder. "I can't see him, but it must be him."

12

After that, for the longest time we kept hearing those scratching and breathing noises. Ben would yell, "Winston – go home!" But the noises kept up. Finally, our eyes started to get heavy and Matt began to snore.

13

SSG111   ISBN: 9781487704001 © On The Mark Press

All of a sudden Ben sits bolt-upright in his sleeping bag. Even in the dark I can see that his eyes were bugged right out.

"What's the matter?" I ask. Now even Matt is wide awake.

"Our dog," Ben says. "I just remembered. My brother took him on a camping trip. He's gone for the week."

We are quiet for a minute, then Matt says in a really soft voice, "What was that noise then?"

Ben and I just look at each other. What was that noise?

14

15

16

17

18

SSG111   ISBN: 9781487704001 © On The Mark Press

Backyard Sleepover: Questions

1. What surprised the narrator in the story about spending the summer at his cousin Ben's house? (paragraph 1)

   ○ He thought it would rain all summer but it was warm and sunny.

   ○ He thought it would be boring but it turned out to be exciting.

   ○ He thought his cousin didn't like him but they became good friends.

   ○ He thought the house had a huge yard but it was very small.

2. When did the boys build the treehouse? (paragraph 2)

   ○ the first day

   ○ the first weekend

   ○ the first week

   ○ the first month

3. In paragraph 3, what does the word "excitable" mean when used to describe Matt?

   ○ someone who is very calm

   ○ someone who is easily excited

   ○ someone who never gets excited

   ○ someone who likes to have fun

4. Why are Matt and Ben whispering in paragraphs 7 and 8?

   ○ They don't want Ben's parents to hear them.

   ○ They are afraid when they hear the scratching sound.

   ○ They can't talk any louder.

   ○ They are very tired.

Backyard Sleepover: Questions

5. What does the word "whimper" mean in paragraph 10?

   ○ a weak, crying sound

   ○ a loud cough

   ○ a nervous laugh

   ○ a high voice

6. In paragraph 12, Ben crawls to the side of the treehouse to

   ○ see if there are ghosts down below.

   ○ call for help.

   ○ look for Matt.

   ○ look for his dog Winston.

7. Why is paragraph 16 important to the story?

   ○ The boys find out Ben's brother went camping.

   ○ The boys find out that Ben has a dog.

   ○ The boys find out that Ben's dog could not be making the noises.

   ○ The boys find out Ben's parents are gone.

8. What can you tell from paragraphs 17 and 18?

   ○ The boys don't know what was making the noises.

   ○ Ghosts were making the noises.

   ○ The boys were dreaming about the noises.

   ○ Ben's brother was making the noises.

SSG111   ISBN: 9781487704001 © On The Mark Press

Backyard Sleepover: Questions

9. Explain why the boys decided to have a sleepover in the backyard. Use details from the text and your own ideas to support your answer.

_____

_____

_____

_____

_____

_____

10. Explain why you think Matt was able to fall asleep that night? Use details from the text and your own ideas to support your answer.

_____

_____

_____

_____

_____

_____

Writing a Paragraph

11. Write a final paragraph for this story. Describe how the boys find out what was making the noises they heard in the night.

Ideas for my paragraph

_____

_____

_____

_____

_____

_____

_____

_____

Write your paragraph on the next page.

This page will not be scored.

 SSG111   ISBN: 9781487704001 © On The Mark Press

Writing a Paragraph

Write your paragraph here. Remember to check your spelling, grammar, and punctuation.

_____

_____

_____

_____

_____

_____

_____

_____

_____

_____

_____

Do not write in this area.

SSG111   ISBN: 9781487704001 © On The Mark Press

Writing Multiple Choice

12. Choose the word or words that correctly completes the sentence.

    This morning, I _____ downstairs to open the front door.

    ○ ran

    ○ will run

    ○ running

    ○ can run

13. Choose the sentence that is written correctly.

    ○ How would you like to go skating, "asked Dad?"

    ○ "How would you like to go skating" asked Dad.

    ○ "How would you like to go skating?" asked Dad.

    ○ "How would you like to go skating!" asked Dad?

14. Which sentence does not belong in the following paragraph?

    (a.) Bats like to fly at night. (b.) That is when they hunt for food. (c.) They like to sleep in the daytime. (d.) Sometimes they live in caves. (e.) Bats hang upside down to sleep.

    ○ Sentence b.

    ○ Sentence c.

    ○ Sentence d.

    ○ Sentence e.

15. Choose the sentence that correctly joins the words "you are."

    ○ Your my friend.

    ○ Youre' going too fast.

    ○ You're the best student in the class.

    ○ Your'e late for school.

SSG111   ISBN: 9781487704001 © On The Mark Press

Writing Multiple Choice

16. Choose the best order to make a paragraph using the following sentences.

    a. It becomes rain before it reaches the ground.
    b. Snow is most likely to be found in high places.
    c. Some mountains are always covered in snow.
    d. Snow often melts as it passes through warmer air.

    ○ d, c, a, b

    ○ b, a, d, c

    ○ b, c, d, a

    ○ c, b, a, d

17. What is the best way to join the following sentences?

    Josh likes to watch basketball.
    Josh likes to play hockey.
    Josh's favorite sport is soccer.

    ○ Josh likes to watch basketball, play soccer and hockey.

    ○ Josh likes to watch basketball and play hockey but his favorite sport is soccer.

    ○ Josh likes basketball soccer and hockey.

    ○ Josh's favorite sports are basketball, soccer, and hockey.

18. Choose the punctuation and word to best complete this sentence.

    "Ouch ____ I cut my finger," _____ Beth.

    ○ ! / said

    ○ ? / asked

    ○ ! / cried

    ○ " / whispered

African Elephants

What are their traits?

African elephants are the largest land animals. Their long trunks are really elongated noses and upper lips. Like most noses, trunks are for smelling. But these "noses" are also for touching and grasping.

Both males and females have tusks. They use their tusks to get food by digging up roots and prying bark off trees.

African elephants have huge, thin ears that help keep them cool in the hot sun. They also use their trunks to keep them cool by spraying a trunk-full of cool water all over their bodies. After their showers, they spray dust all over their bodies like a special kind of elephant sunscreen.

Elephants are social creatures. They sometimes hug by wrapping their trunks together in displays of greeting and affection.

Adult females and their young travel in herds. Adult males generally travel alone or in groups of their own. Elephants can live to be about 70 years old.

SSG111 ISBN: 9781487704001 © On The Mark Press

Where do the live?

African elephants live in the wild on much of the African continent south of the Sahara Desert.

What do they eat?

African elephants are herbivores. They eat mainly roots, leaves, fruit, grasses, and bark. They roam great distances to find enough food. In fact, they spend little time sleeping. They spend most of their time looking for food. One elephant can eat 136 kilograms of food in one day!

What are their babies like?

Elephant babies are born live. They are called calves. Of all animals, elephants have the longest pregnancy – it lasts 22 months!

Elephants usually give birth to one calf every two to four years. At birth, elephants already weigh some 91 kilograms and stand about 1 meter tall.

All the females in the herd help the mother take care of the baby. When a baby is born, the other females gather around and welcome the newborn to the herd.

The baby is dependent on its mother for three to five years. An elephant calf often sucks its trunk for comfort, just as a human baby sucks it thumb!

Who are their enemies?

Because of their size, adult African elephants have no enemies other than humans. Calves, however, may fall prey to lions, crocodiles, and other meat-eaters.

12

What is their connection to humans?

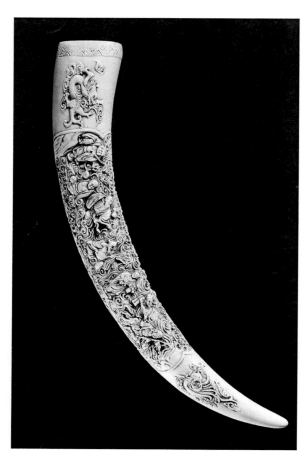

People hunt elephants mainly for their ivory tusks. Ivory is valued by some cultures as a sign of wealth. Carved ivory is often used to make religious objects and works of art. African elephants are mostly wild. Humans do not usually tame these elephants like they do some other kinds of elephants.

13

Are they endangered?

African elephants are considered threatened. Poaching and habitat destruction threaten African elephants throughout their range.

14

SSG111   ISBN: 9781487704001 © On The Mark Press

African Elephants: Questions

1. What does the word "elongated" describe in paragraph 1?

   ○ elephants

   ○ noses and upper lips

   ○ trunks

   ○ land animals

2. What is the main purpose of paragraph 3?

   ○ to describe the elephant's ears

   ○ to tell about elephant sunscreen

   ○ to tell how elephants stay cool and protect themselves from the sun

   ○ to tell about elephant trunks

3. Why do African elephants wrap their trunks together?

   ○ to give each other hugs

   ○ because they travel in herds

   ○ because they are social

   ○ to protect themselves

4. African elephants roam great distances

   ○ to find a place to sleep

   ○ to find enough food to eat

   ○ because they live in Africa

   ○ because they are herbivores

African Elephants: Questions

5. According to paragraph 8, compared to other animals, how are elephants different?

   ○ Their babies are born live.

   ○ They take good care of their babies.

   ○ Their babies are called calves.

   ○ They have the longest pregnancies.

6. What does the word "dependent" mean as used in paragraph 11?

   ○ Elephant babies may or may not be born healthy.

   ○ Elephant babies need their mothers to take care of them.

   ○ Elephant babies need to suck their trunks.

   ○ Elephant babies may or may not live very long.

7. Why do you think humans are the only enemies of African elephants? Use details from the text and your own ideas to support your answer.

   _____

   _____

   _____

   _____

   _____

   _____

 SSG111   ISBN: 9781487704001 © On The Mark Press

African Elephants: Questions

8. Explain what happens when a baby elephant is born. Use details from the text to support your answer.

_____

_____

_____

_____

_____

_____

_____

9. Explain why elephants spend so little time sleeping. Use details from the text and your own ideas to support your answer.

_____

_____

_____

_____

_____

_____

_____

Writing a Story

10. You are invited to go on a trip to Africa. Write an adventure story about your trip and the animals that you see there.

   Ideas for My Story

   _____

   _____

   _____

   _____

   _____

   _____

   _____

   _____

   _____

   _____

Write your story on the next page.

This page will not be scored.

SSG111   ISBN: 9781487704001 © On The Mark Press

Writing a Story

Write your story here. Remember to check your spelling, grammar, and punctuation.

_____

_____

_____

_____

_____

_____

_____

_____

_____

_____

_____

_____

_____

_____

_____

_____

_____

_____

_____

_____

SSG111   ISBN: 9781487704001 © On The Mark Press

Writing Multiple Choice

11. Choose the word that correctly completes the sentence.

   Last week, my big brother Alex _____ me with my math homework.

   ○ helps

   ○ help

   ○ helping

   ○ helped

12. Choose the word that best joins the sentences.

   Alicia doesn't want to get up this morning.
   She didn't sleep very well last night.

   ○ and

   ○ but

   ○ because

   ○ with

13. Choose the sentence that correctly joins the words "could not."

   ○ I wanted to go to the mall today but I couldnt get a ride.

   ○ I wanted to go to the mall today but I couldnt' get a ride

   ○ I wanted to go to the mall today but I could'nt get a ride.

   ○ I wanted to go to the mall today but I couldn't get a ride.

SSG111   ISBN: 9781487704001 © On The Mark Press

How to Take Care of a Puppy

PARAGRAPH

PART 1

Welcoming Your Puppy Home

Make your home puppy safe. Keep all electrical cords out of the puppy's way and close all low windows. Lock away any toxic cleaning supplies or chemicals. Get a folding gate or exercise pen to keep him confined to a certain area. **1**

Make a comfy puppy bed. Choose an area of the house for a day time bed and a night time bed. A warm kitchen or bathroom is a good place for a daytime bed because if he makes a mess the floors are easily washable. **2**

A pillow and blanket or a basket with towels can make a cozy bed. Many people like to use a crate with a pillow and blanket. At night, you might want to keep your puppy in your bedroom so you can hear him and take care of him if it's needed. **3**

PART 2

Affection and Protection

Give your puppy lots of love. It's important to pet your puppy often. Pet him gently on his head, body and legs. This is a great way for you to get to know each other and form a strong bond. **4**

Be careful with your puppy. Hold your puppy gently and pick him up carefully, making sure to keep one hand under his chest. **5**

Keep your puppy safe. When your puppy is outside, make sure to keep an eye on him. He could easily escape from the yard and get lost. It's best if he can play in a fenced yard. Make sure he has a collar with a tag that includes his name and your address and phone number. **6**

PART 3 — Feeding Your Puppy

Choose high-quality, protein rich food. Make sure the food is made specially for puppies. Your vet can recommend a good brand. You will need a bowl for his food and one for water.

Feed him small amounts of food several times a day, depending on his age. At 6 to 12 weeks, he needs to eat 4 times a day. At 3 to 6 months, he needs to eat 3 times a day. At 6 to 12 months, he needs to eat 2 times a day. Make sure he always has clean, fresh water to drink.

7

8

PART 4 — Your Puppy's Health

Find a good vet. One of the first things you should do when you a get a new puppy is take it to the vet to make sure he is healthy. Your vet can give you good advice about feeding and watching for signs of illness.

Keep your puppy's environment safe and clean. Make sure to wash any dirty bedding and clean up any messes right away. Puppies like to chew on things so remove any harmful plants that might make them sick. Also remove any breakable items from the areas where you keep your puppy.

Good grooming helps your puppy stay healthy. Carefully brush him everyday for just a few minutes. As he gets used to being brushed, you can spend more time with him. Have his nails trimmed as needed and keep his teeth clean.

Give your puppy plenty of exercise. Start by taking your puppy on short walks in the yard on leash. Ask your vet when it is safe to take him on walks out of the yard. A total of an hour of walk time a day broken up into several short walks is best.

9

10

11

12

SSG111   ISBN: 9781487704001 © On The Mark Press

PART 3

Training Your Puppy

Start potty training right away! Successfully housebreaking your puppy is one of the most important things to focus on. It will make you're your life much easier. **13**

The first step is paying close attention to when your puppy might need to go potty. The most common times are first thing in the morning, right after eating and drinking, during and after exercise, and right before bedtime. Be sure to praise and reward your puppy each time he goes potty for you outside. **14**

Teach your puppy basic commands. The sooner you start teaching your puppy good habits, the better your relationship will be. A well-behaved puppy is a delight to be around. Start with simple commands like sit, stay, down, and come. Lots of positive reinforcement using treats and affection can be very effective. **15**

Consider a puppy obedience class. The guidance and support of a good obedience class can be very helpful. Classes for puppies usually start at age 4 to 6 months. Your puppy will get to meet and socialize with other puppies which can help prevent behavioural problems down the road. **16**

How to Take Care of a Puppy: Questions

1. Why is it a good idea to put your puppy's daytime bed in a kitchen or bathroom? (paragraph 2)

   ○ There are plenty of towels.

   ○ The rooms are comfortable.

   ○ The floors can be washed easily.

   ○ There are no electrical cords.

2. What does the word "bond" mean as it is used in paragraph 4?

   ○ a good feeling that connects you to your puppy

   ○ something that fastens or holds together

   ○ a contract between you and your puppy

   ○ a promise to pay back money

3. What conclusion can you make from paragraph 6?

   ○ Your puppy should never go outside.

   ○ If your puppy has a collar with a name tag, people can contact you if your puppy gets lost.

   ○ Puppies like to play outside.

   ○ If your puppy gets lost, he will never find his way home.

4. How many times a day should a 4-month old puppy eat?

   ○ 4 times a day

   ○ 2 times a day

   ○ 1 time a day

   ○ 3 times a day

SSG111   ISBN: 9781487704001 © On The Mark Press

How to Take Care of a Puppy: Questions

5. What is the main purpose of paragraph 10?

   ○ To tell you how to keep your puppy's environment safe and clean.

   ○ To tell you how to remove harmful plants.

   ○ To tell you how to clean up messes.

   ○ To tell you what to do if your puppy gets sick.

6. What is the first step in potty training your puppy? (Paragraph 14)

   ○ taking him out first thing in the morning

   ○ giving him lots of praise

   ○ paying close attention to when he might need to go potty

   ○ don't let him eat or drink too much

7. Explain why you think it is important to teach your puppy basic commands. Use details from the text and your own ideas to support your answer.

   _____

   _____

   _____

   _____

   _____

   _____

   _____

How to Take Care of a Puppy: Questions

8. What is one of the most important things to teach your puppy? Use details from the text and your own ideas to support your answer.

_____

_____

_____

_____

_____

_____

9. Explain why you think a puppy obedience class might be a good idea. Use details from the text and your own ideas to support your answer.

_____

_____

_____

_____

_____

_____

SSG111   ISBN: 9781487704001 © On The Mark Press

Writing a Paragraph

10. Write a paragraph about taking care of a pet. Tell what kind of pet it is and name two things you might need to do to take care of it.

Ideas for My Paragraph

_____

_____

_____

_____

_____

_____

_____

_____

_____

Write your paragraph on the next page.

This page will not be scored.

Writing a Paragraph

Write your paragraph here. Remember to check your spelling, grammar, and punctuation.

_____

_____

_____

_____

_____

_____

_____

_____

_____

_____

_____

Do not write in this area.

SSG111   ISBN: 9781487704001 © On The Mark Press

Writing Multiple Choice

11. Choose the word or words that correctly completes the sentence.

    Last month, we _____ six days at the beach.

    ○ will spend

    ○ spending

    ○ spent

    ○ can spend

12. Choose the words that best start and join the following sentence.

    _____ Amy goes for a walk, she will eat lunch _____ she is not very hungry.

    ○ Before / although

    ○ Because / since

    ○ After / and

    ○ When / since

13. Choose the sentence that does not belong in the paragraph below.

    A roadrunner is a funny desert bird. It can run very fast, but it doesn't fly very often. The desert kangaroo rat looks like a gerbil. The roadrunner finds food by chasing insects and little lizards in the desert heat.

    ○ A roadrunner is a funny desert bird.

    ○ It can run very fast, but it doesn't fly very often.

    ○ The desert kangaroo rat looks like a gerbil.

    ○ The roadrunner finds food by chasing insects and little lizards in the desert heat.

Life in a Castle

PARAGRAPH

It's fun to dream about living in a castle but life in a real castle during medieval times was not always so good. If you were rich your life was much better than if you were poor.

1

Here are the stories of two young girls living in the Middle Ages. Lady Isabelle lives in the castle. Agnes works in the castle laundry and lives in rooms above the laundry.

2

Lady Isabelle

Lady Isabelle's family is rich. Her parents own the castle where she and her family live. She is the oldest girl at 12 years old and has two younger sisters. She has learned to read and write from the court teacher.

3

As the oldest, it is her duty to help run the household. She must learn to supervise the cooks and servants, arrange grand feasts, and keep the supplies stocked. She and her family always have plenty of good food to eat.

4

Lady Isabelle wears beautiful clothes made from the finest silks and satins along with expensive jewelry made just for her. She has a maid to help her dress each day. Even with her duties, her life is mostly one of leisure.

5

SSG111   ISBN: 9781487704001 © On The Mark Press

Lady Isabelle attends many fancy parties. She has perfect manners and knows all the latest dances. Within a couple of years, she will marry a wealthy gentleman and have her own family.

6

Agnes

Agnes's family are servants and she is very poor. She lives in small, drafty rooms above the castle laundry with her mother and seven sisters and brothers. Her father died last year.

7

Agnes is 12 years old and the oldest girl in her family. She cannot read or write as she has never had the chance to go to school. Agnes works six long days each week in the laundry and helps out at home on her day off. There is hardly ever any time for relaxation or play.

8

It's hot in the castle laundry and the work is very hard. Agnes has worked there since she was eight. If she is slow doing her work, the head laundress may yell at her or hit her.

9

Agnes wears plain clothes made from rough wool or linen. She and her family are often hungry as they can only afford small amounts of simple food. Agnes dreams of a better life but she will probably marry another servant or boy from the village and be a servant for the rest of her life.

10

Life in a Castle: Questions

1. Why is paragraph 3 important to the story?

   ○ It tells the story of two young girls in medieval times.

   ○ It introduces the reader to Lady Isabelle.

   ○ It describes the castle where the girls live.

   ○ It tells about Lady Isabelle's education.

2. What does the word "leisure" mean as used in paragraph 5?

   ○ a life with lots of free time

   ○ a life that is full of duties

   ○ a life with servants

   ○ a life of grand feasts

3. How will Lady Isabelle's life change in a couple of years?

   ○ She will go to many parties.

   ○ She will plan fancy feasts.

   ○ She will marry a wealthy gentleman.

   ○ She will will get a maid.

4. What has Agnes done since she was eight? (paragraph 9)

   ○ read lots of books

   ○ played in the castle courtyard

   ○ worked in the castle laundry

   ○ worn fine clothes

SSG111   ISBN: 9781487704001 © On The Mark Press

Life in a Castle: Questions

5. Describe what it's like for Agnes at work. Use information from the text and your own ideas to support your answer.

_____

_____

_____

_____

_____

_____

6. Name two ways Lady Isabelle and Agnes are alike and two ways they are different.

_____

_____

_____

_____

_____

_____

SSG111 ISBN: 9781487704001 © On The Mark Press

Writing a Paragraph

7. Imagine that your family won the lottery and you were instantly very rich. Write a paragraph describing some ways that your life would change.

Ideas for My Paragraph

_____

_____

_____

_____

_____

_____

_____

_____

Write your paragraph on the next page.

This page will not be scored.

SSG111   ISBN: 9781487704001 © On The Mark Press

Writing a Paragraph

Write your paragraph here. Remember to check your spelling, grammar, and punctuation.

_____

_____

_____

_____

_____

_____

_____

_____

_____

_____

_____

Do not write in this area.

Punctuation

1. Rewrite the following sentences using the correct punctuation.

    a. Quick Call for an ambulance

    _____

    b. Please Andy will you go outside and play

    _____

    c. This morning I took a shower got dressed and made breakfast

    _____

    _____

    d. Can you keep your appointment today asked Dr Wallace

    _____

    _____

    e. Stop Can't you see that car racing down the street

    _____

    _____

2. Choose the sentence that joins the words "do not" and "who is" correctly.

    ○ I don't know whose supposed to go home first.

    ○ I dont know whos' supposed to go home first.

    ○ I don't know who's supposed to go home first.

    ○ I donot know who's supposed to go home first.

SSG111   ISBN: 9781487704001 © On The Mark Press

Word Usage

3. Sometimes words sound the same but mean different things. Find the word used incorrectly in each sentence, then rewrite the sentences using the correct word.

   a. Their is Mrs. Langley's dog.

   _____

   b. "Come on over hear," yelled the coach.

   _____

   c. You're phone is ringing.

   _____

4. Choose the word that correctly completes the following sentence.

   Last week, Mia _____ cupcakes to school.

   ○ brang

   ○ brought

   ○ bring

   ○ bringed

5. Choose the word that correctly joins the following sentences.

   You better put on your coat. It's pouring down rain.

   ○ and

   ○ but

   ○ since

   ○ with

Contractions

6. Write the contraction for each pair of the following words.

would not _____   I have _____

will not _____   they have _____

she will _____   it is _____

who will _____   we are _____

we would _____   let us _____

Word Endings

7. Add "ed" and "ing" to the following words. Check your spelling carefully.

	ed	**ing**
trust	_____	_____
fail	_____	_____
chase	_____	_____
slice	_____	_____
trip	_____	_____
knit	_____	_____
hum	_____	_____
stir	_____	_____

  SSG111   ISBN: 9781487704001 © On The Mark Press

TEST #1: AN UNEXPECTED VISITOR

1. He needs some help fixing things around the barn.
2. to describe the farm where Gramps lives
3. extremely tired
4. a moose
5. a. The boys arrive in Moosonee after a long train ride.
   e. The moose stands looking at the boys for awhile and then wanders off into the woods.
6. Answers will vary.
7. Answers will vary
8. Butler Acres school is brick and it sits on the corner of Maple and Birch streets.
9. will go
10. I don't know Sara very well.
11. libraries, branches, ladies, lamps, soldiers, addresses, countries
12. The three babies' blankets were each a different color.
13. Sentence b.

TEST #2: BEARS JUST WANT TO HAVE FUN

1. to move in a slow, heavy way
2. to get to the bugs underneath it
3. to describe the picnic food that was on the table
4. at a roadside rest stop
5. The bears are looking for food.
6. He is afraid the bears will hurt the family.
7. Answers will vary.
8. Answers will vary.
9. Answers will vary.
10. when
11. "Get up!" yelled Clark. "You'll be late for school."
12. Then the cubs go off on their own.
13. Help! I can't swim!
14. "Let's go to the movies," said Jane.
15. Shouldn't you try to get home before dark?
16. Maya went to the store to buy eggs, milk, cheese, and bread.
17. Mrs. Wilson asked, "Could you please take my picture?"
18. Yes, Jackie, you can go skating tomorrow.

TEST #3: WHAT IS A MAMMAL?

1. the mammals' body temperature.
2. to explain why mammals have hair or fur on their bodies
3. qualities that belong to and help to identify all mammals
4. platypus and echidna
5. Most baby mammals will die if they are not cared for.
6. They spend several weeks in their mother's pouch.
7. Answers will vary.
8. alike: both mammals, live young
   different: horses born able to walk, mice barely able to crawl, horses covered with hair, mice born hairless, horses born with eyes and ears open, mice born with eyes and ears shut
9. They learn to survive intense tropical heat and freezing arctic temperatures.
10. Answers will vary.
11. bought / but
12. "When the class is over, let's go outside," said Meg.
13. c, a, d, b

TEST #4: PARTS OF AN AIRPLANE

1. the parts of the airplane
2. at the back of the plane
3. fuselage
4. propellers and wings
5. The rudder is on the tail, when you move it right or left the nose of the plane moves in the same direction.
6. The flaps on the wing can be raised or lowered to create lift or drag, helping the plane during takeoff and landing.
7. Stories will vary.
8. It rains almost everyday.
9. Before

TEST #5: LIFE CYCLE OF A MONARCH BUTTERFLY

1. butterfly egg
2. Its appearance changes as it grows and sheds its skin.
3. all the time
4. four to six days
5. after the cocoon is formed
6. It breaks out of the cocoon.
7. the cocoon is being formed, the butterfly is breaking out of the cocoon
8. Answers will vary.
9. The father gorilla makes his bed on the ground.
10. We like to watch the fireworks in our town on New Years Eve, but we don't like the noise.
11. took, to
12. Please stand behind the yellow line.
13. b, d, c, a

TEST #6: BACKYARD SLEEPOVER

1. He thought it would be boring but it turned out to be exciting.
2. the first week
3. someone who is easily excited
4. They are afraid when they hear the scratching sound.
5. a weak, crying sound
6. look for his dog Winston.
7. The boys find out that Ben's dog could not be making the noises.
8. The boys don't know what was making the noises.
9. Answers will vary
10. Answers will vary
11. Answers will vary
12. ran
13. "How would you like to go skating?" asked Dad.
14. Sentence d.
15. You're the best student in the class.
16. b, c, d, a
17. Josh likes to watch basketball and play hockey but his favorite sport is soccer.
18. ! , cried

TEST #7: AFRICAN ELEPHANTS

1. noses and upper lips
2. to tell how elephants stay cool and protect themselves from the sun
3. to give each other hugs
4. to find enough food to eat
5. They have the longest pregnancies.
6. Elephant babies need their mothers to take care of them
7. Answers will vary.
8. All the female elephants welcome the baby and help take care of it.
9. They spend most of their time looking for food.
10. Answers will vary.
11. helped
12. because
13. I wanted to go to the mall today but I couldn't get a ride.

TEST #8: HOW TO TAKE CARE OF A PUPPY

1. The floors can be washed easily.
2. a good feeling that connects you to your puppy
3. If your puppy has a collar with a name tag, people can contact you if he gets lost.
4. 3 times
5. To tell you how to keep your puppy's environment safe and clean.
6. paying close attention to when he might need to go potty
7. to create a good relationship with your puppy and keep him safe
8. Answers will vary.
9. You get guidance and support and your puppy gets socialized.
10. Answers will vary.
11. spent
12. Before, although
13. The desert kangaroo rat looks like a gerbil.

TEST # 9: LIFE IN A CASTLE

1. It introduces the reader to Lady Isabelle.
2. a life with lots of free time
3. She will marry a wealthy gentleman.
4. worked in the castle laundry
5. Answers will vary
6. Answers will vary.
7. Answers will vary.

TEST #10: LANGUAGE SKILLS

1. a. Quick! ambulance.
   b. Please, Andy, play?
   c. morning, shower, dressed, breakfast.
   d. "Can today?" Dr. Wallace. e. Stop! street?
2. I don't know who's supposed to go home first.
3. a. There b. here c. Your
4. brought
5. since
6. wouldn't, won't, she'll, who'll, we'd, I've, they've, it's we're, let's
7. trusted, trusting, failed, failing, chased, chasing, sliced, slicing, tripped, tripping, knitted, knitting, hummed, humming, stirred, stirring

SSG111   ISBN: 9781487704001 © On The Mark Press